2 dos papas redonditas

3

tres kiwis peluditos

4 cuatro bananas amarillas

5 **cinco** manzanas brillantes

6 seis trozos grandes de brócoli

7 siete naranjas jugosas

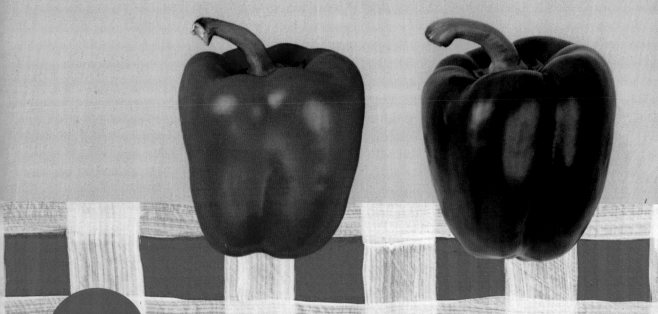

8 **ocho** pimientos
muy dulces

9

nueve tomates sabrosos

10 **diez** melocotones gorditos

Una sandía bien fría

Please visit our Web site at: www.garethstevens.com
For a free color catalog describing Gareth Stevens Publishing's
list of high-quality books and multimedia programs, call
1-800-542-2595 (USA) or 1-800-387-3178 (Canada).
Gareth Stevens Publishing's fax: (414) 332-3567.

Library of Congress Cataloging-in-Publication Data

Tofts, Hannah.
  (One cool watermelon. Spanish)
  Una sandía bien fría / Hannah Tofts; photography by Rupert Horrox.
    p. cm.
  ISBN-13: 978-0-8368-7489-1 (lib. bdg.)
  ISBN-13: 978-0-8368-8144-8 (softcover)
  1. Counting—Juvenile literature. I. Horrox, Rupert, ill. II. Title.
QA113.T65518   2007
513.2'11—dc22
                           2006030679

This edition first published in 2007 by
Gareth Stevens Publishing
A Member of the WRC Media Family of Companies
330 West Olive Street, Suite 100
Milwaukee, Wisconsin 53212 USA

Gareth Stevens editor: Dorothy L. Gibbs
Gareth Stevens art direction and design: Tammy West
Spanish Translation: Tatiana Acosta and Guillermo Gutiérrez

Printed in the United States of America

1 2 3 4 5 6 7 8 9 10 10 09 08 07 06

Una sandía bien fría

Hannah Tofts

Fotografía por Rupert Horrox

GARETH**STEVENS**
GS
PUBLISHING
A Member of the WRC Media Family of Companies

En mi cocina tengo...

una sandía bien fría

¡y me los comería todos!